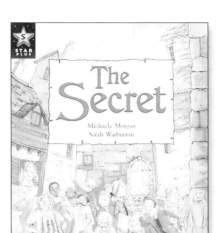

The front cover

Where is the story set?

Who is the main character in the story?

What do you think he does for a living?

What other characters do you think might be in the story?

The back cover

Let's read the blurb together.

Is it hard to keep a secret?

Do you think the little barber will find it hard?

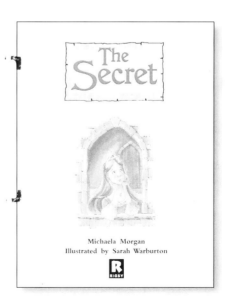

The title page

Who do you think this character is?

Lesson 1 (Chapter 1)

READ

Read pages 2 to 5

Purpose: To find out what the queen's secret was.

PAUSE

Pause at page 5

Why didn't the queen tell anyone her secret?

How does the author describe a secret? (*a heavy, heavy thing*) What do you think this means?

What can you say about the layout of this story? (*the story is carried on through the speech bubbles*)

Chapter 1

There once was a queen.
She was good.
She was brave.
She was rich.
She was beautiful.
And she was happy . . .
except for one thing.
She had a secret.

A secret is a heavy, heavy thing. It weighs on your head and it weighs on your heart. So, even though this queen was a good queen, she was often unhappy.

Her people loved her. They said:

She always knows when WE are unhappy and then she helps.

She always listens to us.

Sometimes she seems so sad. I wish we could cheer her up.

This was her secret: her ears were very different from most people's. The queen didn't like being different from everybody else. She thought to herself, "If people know about these ears of mine, they will point at me and laugh."

She could only imagine what they would say.

Rabbit head!

Big ears!

Ha! Ha!

Donkey ears!

So, when she went out, the queen often wore a hat. She wore all sorts of hats. People *did* point at her. They said:

What a fantastic hat!

What a fine hat!

What an unusual hat!

Look at that!

READ

Read pages 6 to 7

Purpose: To discover the problem in the story.

PAUSE

Pause at page 7

How will the queen get her hair cut and still keep her secret?

Can you suggest ways to solve the queen's problem?

The queen had never let anybody cut her hair, in case they found out her secret.

Often, she had unusual hairstyles. People would say:

Amazing!

What an unusual hairstyle!

Fantastic!

As the years went by, the queen's hair grew longer . . .

and longer . . .

and longer!

Finally, she decided it was TOO long. "I will just have to get it cut," she said.

6

7

READ

Read pages 8 to 11

Purpose: To find out how the queen solved her problem.

PAUSE

Pause at page 11

Did the hairdressers know whose hair they were going to cut? (*ensure the children have read the poster on page 8*)

What was one advantage of having different ears?

How did the queen decide which hairdresser to choose?

The queen put up some posters. Soon, barbers and hairdressers came from all over the land.

They stood outside the castle, and this is what they did:

With the help of her very different ears, the queen listened to them.

8

9

This is what she heard:

There was just one man who didn't join in the gossip. So the queen sent her servant to fetch him.

10

11

READ

Read pages 12 to 13

Purpose: To find out if the barber discovered the queen's secret.

PAUSE

Pause at page 13

What does the queen make the little barber promise? Pick out the exact words from the text.

Please turn to page 16 for Revisit and Respond activities.

When the queen told the barber what he was to do, he was very pleased to have got such an important job.

"I can't wait to tell my wife and children that I am the queen's barber!"

"No!" said the queen. "If you want this job, you must keep it a secret. Promise me you'll never tell a living soul."

The little barber promised, although it was hard to keep such happy news to himself.

The little barber began to cut the queen's hair. *Snip! Snip! Snippety-snip!* went his scissors.

Then – "OH MY!" gasped the little barber. "Look what I've found!"

"Shh." said the queen. "Remember your promise. You mustn't tell a living soul."

12

13

9

Lesson 2 (Chapter 2)

RECAP

Recap lesson 1

What is making the queen sad?

Will the little barber tell anybody the queen's secret?

READ

Read pages 14 to 19

Purpose: To find out if the little barber told the secret.

PAUSE

Pause at page 19

Why is it so difficult for the barber to keep the secret? (*refer to and discuss the term 'open man'*)

Do you think the barber broke his promise to the queen? Why, or why not?

How does the author tell us that the problem isn't over? (. . . *but not for long.*)

Chapter 2

The little barber kept the promise, although it weighed heavily on him. A secret is a heavy weight to carry.

The little barber was an open man, but now he had to be careful about talking to his friends, and careful about talking to his family.

14

"Cheer up!" his wife said. "Tell us all about your day."

The little barber sighed and hung his head. Day after day he kept the secret, and day after day it seemed heavier.

15

One day, the little barber was walking by the fields on his way to the palace. The sun was shining brightly and all around him the flowers were opening. The birds were singing and the long grass was whispering. Bees buzzed to each other.

It seemed that all the flowers, all the insects, and even the trees and the grass were wide awake and talking to each other.

The little barber felt *so* weighed down by the secret he was keeping. He sat down at the side of a stream, and even the water seemed to be babbling and chattering. He thought about his promise.

"I cannot tell a living soul," he thought, "but I could tell *something!*"

So he whispered to the water reeds:

> The queen has a secret, and it worries her. She thinks the people won't love her if they find out she is different. Her ears are very different from other people's.

The tall reeds and the tall grasses nodded as if they understood. The water went *shush, shush,* as if to soothe him. The sunbeams patted his back as if to say, "There, there. We are glad you can talk to us."

The little barber felt so much better after telling the secret! Now he had a smile on his face and a spring in his step . . . but not for long.

READ

Read pages 20 to 21

Purpose: To find out how the queen's secret was told.

PAUSE

Pause at page 21

How will the people react?

Do you think the queen will punish the barber?
Find evidence in the story to support your answer.
(*she is a good queen*)

A few days later, when the little barber arrived at the palace, he saw a woman selling little pipes. The pipes were made out of reeds – the very same reeds that knew the secret!

The woman started playing the pipes. They sang out:

♪ We've got a secret we can share.
We know what's under your queen's hair.
We know you love your queen so dear.
So why not love her different ears?

"Oh, no!" thought the little barber.
"Oh, no!" thought the queen, and she looked at the people. Already, they were pointing and laughing and talking about her.

20

21

READ

Read pages 22 to the end

Purpose: To find out how the people behave towards the queen.

PAUSE

Pause at page 24

How does the queen feel about her ears at the end of the story?

In what way is this book like other traditional tales?

Then the queen listened. This is what the people were saying:

Maybe that is why she is such a good listener!

How unusual our queen is!

How fantastic!

How special!

How amazing!

22

The queen smiled. Now, at last, she understood.

"It wasn't being different that made me unhappy. It was keeping a secret for all these years that made me feel so sad!"

She looked at the barber and all her people. "I feel much better now. I should have known my ears were special. But I do have one more promise I want everyone to make. I want you to . . .

23

live happily ever after!"
And that is what they all did!

24

After Reading

Revisit and Respond

Lesson 1

T) Ask the children to say how they think the story will continue.

T) What does 'gossip' mean? Ask the children to role play gossiping in pairs.

W) Ask the children to find the word 'trustworthy' on the poster on page 8. Can they think of other words that mean the same?

W) Ask the children to make a list of compound words beginning with 'hair'. (*hairdresser, hairbrush, hairstyle, hairnet*)

Lesson 2

T) Ask the children to find words and phrases that tell us what sort of person the queen was. (e.g. *good listener, helps people*)

W) Think of words to describe the queen's character. (*helpful, caring, inventive, kind*)

T) Prepare the children to compare this story with another *Star Plus* story: *The Mystery of Mrs Kim*. Draw up a chart to describe the story – type of story, setting, main theme/lesson, e.g.

Title	The Secret	The Mystery of Mrs Kim
Type of story	traditional tale	
Setting	imaginary place	
Theme/lesson	don't judge people by appearances	